The Broken Meadow

by Temple Cone

2010 OLD SEVENTY CREEK PRESS
POETRY SERIES AWARD WINNER

COPYRIGHT 2010 BY RUDY THOMAS

2010 OLD SEVENTY CREEK FIRST EDITION
PRINTED IN THE UNITED STATES OF AMERICA

PUBLISHED IN THE UNITED STATES
BY OLD SEVENTY CREEK PRESS
RUDY THOMAS, PUBLISHER
P. O. BOX 204
ALBANY, KENTUCKY 42602

ISBN: **1451526075**
EAN: **9781451526073**

PRINTED BY CREATE SPACE FOR
OLD SEVENTY CREEK PRESS

For Shannon and Isabelle

CONTENTS

ACKNOWLEDGMENTS

The author gratefully acknowledges the editors of the publications in which these poems first appeared:

Aethlon: The Journal of Sports Literature: "Mercy"

Best Modern Voices: Words for the New Millennium: "A Whispered Change"

The Flea: "Nettles"

Free Verse: "Finding the Words," "Heron"

Hawk & Whippoorwill: "Cord"

Minnetonka Review: "Blessing," "A Filament of Proof"

Off the Coast: "Cleansing"

Plain Spoke: "A Prayer in the Fields"

Poem: "The Basket"

Sow's Ear Poetry Review: "The Minor Angel"

Tar River Poetry: "Two Trees"

"Epithalamion with Charles Mingus's *Black Saint and the Sinner Lady* Playing Through It" won the 2009 Utmost Christian Writers April Poetry Contest.

Several haiku in "Saving Daylight" first appeared in *Acorn, Daily Haiku, Frogpond, Mayfly,* and *Modern Haiku.*

Some of the poems here appeared in the chapbook *Quandary Farm* (Pudding House, 2008).

The sky is cut out for accepting prayers.

– James Galvin

For the Better Angel

I am going down to the river,
its low flats and bleary dawns.
Join me, if you will,
or linger on the banks awhile
where the sad shadows of childhood
keep dew from burning away,
where the watermen launch out
before the aubade of blackbirds
to gather crab traps
with hands that ache so
from clutching chill ropes
they'll give you a nickel
for a bag of caught honeybees
whose stings, they say, lighten the pain.
I am going someplace deep down
where the children I knew,
nameless now,
pull me into the water,
splashing, laughing, sousing
me in a moment of holiness
without suffering. O angel,
you may not have forgotten me,
but you'll never know me
if this shore isn't first your own.
Fifty steps from door to wharf,
mockingbirds in the catalpa
and coolness of crickets under the porch.
The river's name means *slow water*,
but you know the name of every river
really means *the river of death*,
which we all cross over.
                              Listen now,
I'm going down to this place
to find the boy I can't recall growing from,
this boy who might be crying now
or laughing, God only knows.
Even if he's gone, even if I get lost,

I've got to go down to that river.
Come with me. I can't come up to you.

Beginning

Nothing will touch you as lightly
as walking mid-October through a field
of chicory, blown milkweed, aster and cornflower
into a woods of red-needled pine
you know gives way to second-growth.

Snapped twigs clinging
to shirtsleeves like children,
half-glint of mockingbird in the undershade,
you move through bracken, nettles,
the quiet draws and hills.

And before you see them,
filaments of web drift across your face
like worn threads of a shawl,
silk dressings someone has wrapped
over your wounded eyes.

Nettles

Tests of bravery, they were, thick-set clusters
of glassy ooze drifting with river tides,
Trojans rallying at Hector's muster
to strike any who crossed the plain (or tried).

Their stings were worse than death's dart. A poultice
of wet sand was triage, of salt the cure.
From the wharf, I'd watch for them to surface,
count, then make a choice: swim or stay ashore.

But my father taught me to grip the bloom
of pulsing jelly comb, to draw out ghosts
from black brackwater and then entomb
them in sand or lay them on planks to roast,

incandesce, and vanish in the scorching air.
I understood men did this. I, too, could dare.

Cleansing

He holds the trout in his hands,
a loaf of shimmering bread. Should he
let it drown in the burning air
or stun it against the rock,
a hard blow before he guts it whole?
The task, like so many, is simple,
but not the choice. Pines sway on
the cliffs overhead, sun glints
along the edge of his buckknife,
and for a second he loses the river,
the trout, even his hand in a star's glare.
When he grips again, a last pulse
clenches the tail, flings water in his eyes.
Then he feels the quiet enter his palm.

For V.P. Loggins

Blessed

When Wes Harmon shot me
with his .22,
I knew I was dead
and lay in the dust, crying.
I didn't hear song, didn't see
much but flickering shapes
at the edge of dry light.
Wes's face was a shadow
when he picked me up;
the rabbit had been
so fixed in his sights
he forgot I'd wandered ahead.
We fingered the tear
in my shirt, marking ourselves
with the blood of mistakes.
Years since, I trace
the smooth nick of flesh,
remind myself
that heaven is this place, this pain.

Swimming Haunts

Once, my father fished me out a lake
I nearly drowned in. I'd been rowing, alone,
and went in after an oar that slid from its lock
while I'd been watching a bittern in the shallows.
Just twelve, I treaded water what seemed like hours.
From knees to groin, my legs burned, the pulse
of each kick diminishing as I hung there
in watery light that darkened below.

Years later, following a trail of switchbacks
cut like ritual scars along a mountain,
I tracked a series of falls to their source,
a deep pool I decided I had to swim,
to touch bottom, to feel my lungs burn
like his words when he raised me from the lake.

Cooper's Hawk

Up high a Cooper's hawk, done chasing doves
all morning, mounts lazily the columns
of heat summer earth projects. It loves
the rough spiral the desperate height sends
it after, tracing and tracing the unseen,
to face the sun till sunset makes it stop.
Below, gray rabbits scatter through a screen
of withered brake. The hawk angles up
the round only time grants, only time cleaves,
hunger powering flight as much as wind.
Interstices between stars run eons:
this moment gleams miles through the misery
of ploughed down pines, plainlands seared to sand.
One life outshines light from a thousand suns.

Heron

It wakes facing east and turns west at night,
great wings no heavier than a creek stone.
By looking, it prepares a deeper sight.

Over its still feathers, ripples of light.
A marsh wind stirs dry rushes like bones.
It wakes facing east and turns west at night.

No owl's as sudden, silent, when the white
pickerel flashes near shore, a slivered moon.
By looking, it prepares a deeper sight.

The way the serpent-neck crooks back in flight
recalls curved fossils of birds long gone.
It wakes facing east and turns west at night

towards the line where dim blues and grays form late.
Ghost hues match the folded wings, tone for tone.
By looking, it prepares a deeper sight.

Nesting high in cottonwoods, they mate
in pairs, but have to pass long winters alone.
Each wakes facing east and turns west at night.
By looking, they prepare a deeper sight.

Behest

Long before day, the birds awake
for their own sake, but not to play.
Whether in spring, summer, or fall,
the sparrows brawl and cardinals sing
while dark stays deep as midnight.
Whatever sun might warm wings lies
beyond the range of shifting eyes,
though blackness frays, revealing strange
cracks and seams of branches, and almost
seems composed of other substance
than the lack of light. It is not hope
that wakes them, though perhaps delight,
too human a word, misses the grief
and the relief felt as each bird
rattles its nest, frail wicker boat,
and with clear notes sings at dawn's behest.

Out in the Dark

The dusk was all the swallows had
to see them home by dark.
The summer in the forest leaves
had not been shed, though bark

on one sycamore gleamed halfway
and made me think of snow.
But I chose not to dwell on that
far-off cold, even though

the woods themselves were readying.
Here and there a thrush rang
from deep within the undergrowth,
as if the dawn it sang

were not already hours past,
as if the clouded stars
weren't shining when a warm breeze passed.
I couldn't help but shiver.

Then all was gone—swallows, thrush, stars—
and night at last had come.
It meant staying still a while
or heading home for some.

A Whispered Change

The trees began to whisper
a change was coming soon.

Cold winds chased after
leaves, dropped forests by noon,

while the names of birds flew
all night, like memory,

leaving but jay and crow
to tell what birds could be.

Soon even the light had gone,
like the thought of green, away.

Yet when the night stars shone
or frost glistened by day,

something whispered, *Winter ends.*
Still, the hastening geese

might have been forgiven
their doubts that dark would cease,

that earth would find release.

Vesper

The silent woods in shadow,
then the leafy floor turns white
as cold and steady winds blow
clouds from the moon tonight.
Silver all around us,
silver grass on silver fields,
silver on your upturned face;
such beauty silver yields.
The streets are streams of starshine.
A wren calls out, beguiled
by this sudden second sun
that leaves the night unveiled.
Now while we walk in silver
light, let's not forget: days
to a bird may last forever,
but we know nothing stays.

Prayer

In the field the frost set, to the fence and low pines,
back over the field the hawk clawed a dove.
When they fell together, touched by God, I was amazed
I was there, keeping vigil over the chill cooing.
Then the hawk shuddered, or was it the dove
shuddering beneath exquisite talons,
which even now are tearing skin, my God, flesh,
plucking, stripping dark strings of muscle, tendon, viscera,
before reaching the bones, clean and mathematical.
Only you know this is how it is,
this is prayer, only this and then the hard whiteness.

Cord

The deer in that beautiful place lay down their bones. I must wear
mine.
                         – Robinson Jeffers

The two who'd brought him left over the rise,
lurching through withered stalks of goldenrod and
      foxglove,
the long rifles branching from their shoulders.

He heard their gumboots fret the dew-sotted grass,
a thick-quilled beast crossing the field for the purlieu
of the woods, or ghosts holding the night in place.

Soon gray light broke hard and clear to his right, a cusp
illuminating the line of earth. So the long watch began.
He breathed slow while crickets shutter-clicked nearby,

predawn cold pulling him back to a dully remembered
      place,
then turned into the woods, hands outstretched,
touch-walking through small pines till he reached a poplar

in the clearing. He found the ladder nailed to the trunk,
mounted, reached into the limbs like a child who waits to
      be lifted,
each plank a signpost on a path no one would pass.

The outer leaves were rimed with wasp-papery frost that
      crinkled,
then melted under his fingertips. He found the case in a
      bough,
the cartridge box in a rough bole, cardboard mushy from
      the damp.

Thirty cold points. The sky now fired faint sapphire,
and a shook branch sprayed dew on his neck as the sharp
      angle

of a nighthawk's wings crossed the open air and
 disappeared.

Had the forms not shifted below, he might never have
 known
morning passed. One hoof scraped a log. In the quivering
 pause,
he woke to find his hand already dropping the bolt in
 place.

Ahead of two does, the buck pressed, spectral as mercury
 dust.
A rotten chaplet garlanded the dozen points of its antlers
and whisked against its bowed skull. He couldn't believe

their thickening coats, heavy ribs, the way black eyes
sucked in the whole world, so he began counting,
believing a pattern would catch the small gear of history

turning in his heart. When the buck ghosted past the tree,
he rose stiffly to his knees, smelling the musky fur,
keeping sight of the clearing edge where they'd turn their
 flanks.

He clutched the stock against his shoulder, worked it into
 his flesh.
Then the buck was gone, and he dropped from the stand,
circling out, a ripple. The blood trail began fifty feet in.

Eyes lowered, he read the black spills steaming from
 leaves,
felt his own blood course when the spoor darkened,
left the trail whenever it lightened, crossing and crossing
 his path.

The quiet touched him through limbs and webs, blinding
sunlight amid shadow. He heard his own ragged breath,
then the buck's soft blowing as it leaned against an oak,

trying to right itself, gray numbles coiled in the twigs.
He slid back the bolt, hoping he'd chambered another
    round,
but knew, as one knows an unseen fracture, he had not,

then made himself walk close, made himself believe
the buck rose on strong legs, there were no looped guts,
only a cord, weathering in the brush, a strand of
    cellophane,

not the pulse and shit of this live deer whose skull he stove
until his hands bled from the clenched rifle sights.
He dreamt the buck flew. Yes, it flew. Then he was gone,

running two miles through fields to a creek's edge,
his breath glistening, the water buffed obsidian,
wrinkling in eddies along low rocks midstream.

In the chill he wondered how easy it was to surrender,
as someone did each winter, to the lull of cold.
He'd heard of old drunks frozen to statues in the woods,

of coal-miners' widows who left their fires unstoked.
Such loneliness, a storm that blew open the door
of the heart, letting in snow and wind and the night.

So when the men began calling across the creek,
his breath came quick, a cord bridling his mouth,
bit and bridle of song, sweetbitter bond of mastery.

The Owl in the Snow

A barn owl shuts its eyes to the snow.
        Perched at one end of a covered bridge,
                it huddles on a beam,

a lantern left to burn back the dark
        from birches and iced-over elms.
                In the absence of wind,

flakes descend in a wet patter,
        until the bridge seems nothing
                but a part of the woods,

a trunk fallen across the creek-bed.
        When the owl shakes out its wings,
                the sudden stir is an angel's arrival.

Black eyes gleam. Over muskrat and hare,
        snow continues to fall, erasing
                tracks scattered like drops of blood.

The owl gathers itself to cross
        the path the creek cuts through the trees,
                bobs once, silently, then leaps.

Snowbound

The trees stand grave under burdens of snow,
like ghosts death has undone, row after row,
and I'm walking the woods again, alone.
A cherished hour, this, though perhaps not one
which many would wish to find themselves in,
say what they will about the bliss, the blessing
solitude brings. Now each sense is awake
to sense's absence—the silver-black lake
chill and empty as interstitial space,
bare paths like lines shaping an unseen face,
even the iron tang of snow, sharp, then lost.
Thoughts of my own end come and go with frost.
Then, from a fir, a cardinal shakes free,
loosening the snow that settles down on me.

Winter Doubts

Do not doubt but that the crows
speak of winter nights and year's end.
Those who have felt the cold, seen snows,
can sense a change in the autumn wind.

When two or three gather in a tree,
jostling clumsily to make room
on a bare branch, their raw calls leave
you feeling chill, wondering if the gloom

will give way to spring's early light.
But do not shun them. Do not ignore.
Their task, though it bring no delight,
is to help us, by contrast, adore

the pearl moon in its ebony sky.
Ours is but to love and not ask why.

The Minor Angel

A to Z. The boy at his primer knows
the sound each letter makes. The fluted J;
M warming the cheek bones with the broken hum
of a furnace; O, S, and T, the chance given Eve
to pick from fruit-boughs a sweet sweeter than milk-
sopped Oreos. But the sounds seem so many,
the letters wrapped like crepe or tinsel strands
around a Christmas-pine of sense, the tree
so bright, the boy can barely read his name—
an angel's silhouette in brass
that catches the Yule fire's light, turns, like the key
of an aria, in the locked door of the heart,
and glitters with praise. The words, gifts laid out
by the hearth the night before, he leaves untouched,
all but one. Enough, it is, to look and guess
at bows and ribbons (for him!) chosen with love.
From the opened box, he lifts an ornament
to place beside his own: in lettered gold,
the tiny word, *Adore.*

For Penny Livesay

A Filament of Proof

A filament of proof is heaven's law.
The blue sky ruled with clouds, an ant's thorax,
or chiming dolphins undersea imply
cosmos out of chaos, a sort of purpose

indecipherable as tattooed henna.
Wrench an atom open, there lie the quarks
lodged tight as seeds within the grainy
fruit our ancient mother Eve, nervous

and alone, tasted, and made a vessel
for the seasons and our mortality.
Each article of faith is but a guess
we buckle tight as armor, and believe

without backing, though some days, the rattle
of kingfishers could almost bless us all.

The Wind Today

The wind that stirs the fields today
tomorrow turns waves far away,
and outpacing the ocean's tide
shakes aspens by the riverside.

On our cheeks we feel the change itself,
blowing out beyond the dark gulf
of starless night. It is a breath
half-easeful as the thought of death

when we grow tired of men, deeds, love.
We are boats in a silent cove,
drifting ashore. The pale-ribbed sands
clutch us like a father's hands,

who lost us once, never again.
The day is washed by steady rain,
and we await, till breezes shirr,
a voice calling from the river.

Song

Spider-web rickshaws
shiver in the low, damp field,
while white-throated sparrows
spin notes in the trees.
All winter I followed a path
beside deep woods,
snow passing through stripped
branches. Now grass grows
over dirt crescented
with footprints. The insistent
poplars shake out their wings.

Finding the Words

A dry wind sifts tassels
in the field nearby. Out late, walking
the road after a day's work,
I hear nighthawks pitch and chirr,
the air shagged with moths.
By now, deer have stirred from the grass,
rising on legs of twilight and bone,
their steps the patter of rain.
They wait a few heartbeats away
for a breath to set them flying.

After "After Apple-Picking"

Green branches sag with loads of apples
any wind will topple. Their rust-red skins
are flecked like sunlit river shallows,
and that famous pointed ladder's there still,

but I'm no farmer. Though my home's miles deep
in the country, deeper than this orchard,
if I'm to work at picking, it's by choice,
the hot sun on my shirt a welcome pleasure.

The orchard keeper's small shack stands nearby
with its callus of whitewash peeling from the walls
and a broken window stuffed with rags.
Above the freighted trees, swallows curlicue

and from far off comes an oriole's glistening call.
Apple-gaff and basket in hand, I feel halfway
ridiculous, but at peace. I share nothing
with those men who have to tend the apples

all year. At most, I'm a sojourner here,
walking through the wrong groves. I can't even name
the apples I've picked, can't tell the windfall
scent of loss from the juice drying on my hands.

East of the Blue Ridge, West of the Dawn

3 a.m., moon magnificent in her pearl-and-lace.
Dog-eared, clothbound *Cloud of Unknowing* on my chest.

They say a beam of light descends
through the dark like a dropped match.
Its whispers kindle in us
the faith that keeps faith in faith,
fragrant as burning heartwood.

Maybe. But here the moon makes a grail
of the sycamore.
                        Crows high in the branches
gleam like a negative of stars,
beaks thrust in the collars of their wings.
Snow falling, they look on
as the shadow of white rides over.

Grave Rubbing

Hung from a pegboard wall
with wren-houses, shears, barometers,
a gravestone's charcoal rubbing,
the page a sail breath
could rise into. Translucence–
gray thumb-prints visible
on the other side, a tear
in the paper someone taped shut.
The letters stood unsmudged:

Emily Dickinson
Born, December 10, 1830
Returned, May 15, 1886.

Not departure. Return. How else
would it be written?
Her name rubbed with dust,
volcanic flower
crystallized in a fall of ash.

Eastern Easter Eclogue

In and out the locust's branches,
a thorny crucifix just waiting to happen,
waxwings thread and jostle,
                                a backyard hoedown,
their songlessness the playlist
                                of bare ruined choirs.

Mid-spring Shenandoah,
                        soft breast of the mountains
splashed with sunset champagne,
me in a deck chair, awaiting the landscape's cabaret,
how she lifts her silks and slides them back,
appreciatively, on.

Whunk, whunk.
Someone's pitching horseshoes
with little luck,
                    sweet tang and char
of barbeque on the air, honky-tonk incense,
burnt offering of our no-name desires.

If only we knew where we were heading,
Holy Land or Graceland,
                        if only we knew
whether yon landscape
                        were inscape or escape.
If only we'd listened to instructions.

Breezy-wheezy-wheeze, go the waxwings,
still trying to find a song,
the berry marks on their wings burning low
as the last briquette on the grill.
Clouds cast down their sunbeams,
fishing lines of the divine.

A Prayer in the Fields

Tall grass yields like waves before a prow,
blond tassels touching my sleeves. I listen
for meadowlarks: a shirr, then bright wings
floating far downfield. Pebbles gouge my feet.
Near the barn, a calf begins to low,
hard, lonely cries. Already evening
changes stems to long shadows,
day's heat drifts from the ground.
May this day come again. May a light
rain fall, and the clean scent of clover sift
through the open windows at night.

Mercy

I've never told anyone this story.
My first year in college, I tried out at running back
for the varsity football team. Small, swift,

I was dead the moment I skirted a hit
during preseason Oklahomas, the ball grasped
tight to my side, the tackler clutching footsteps.

By summer's end, they'd say I heard footsteps,
though you can't blame me. When he heard the story
of what I'd done, coach called a D-end, grasped

the tusk of his mask, and ordered him back
to where I was larking, to give me the hit
I'd forgotten to take. The guy was swift,

one of those puma-like linemen, so swift
as could be, I found myself on the ground, footsteps
dancing in my head, my mask cracked from the hit.

I should have quit right there, but I needed the story
of how I survived a year at running back.
For whom? For my father, maybe, who had grasped

me hard when I said I wanted to grasp
this chance like the ball on a draw, running swift
past the rush and up the center's back.

Maybe I just feared guilt's footsteps
on my pillow at night, or believed no story
could end with me thrown down. But that hit

made me ease up on runs, soften with each hut
of the cadence. Speed slipped from my grasp
easy as a girl's hair, and I found myself telling stories

about ghost bruises and phantom pulls. I wasn't swift;
I was scared. One day, hearing the trainer's footsteps,
I dropped during drills and faked a thrown back.

I knew I was done. My feet trudged slowly back
to the locker-room, the air inside so cold it hit
harder than the blow I tried to slip. Now I step

back from this shame, finding I can't grasp
the boy I was, even though I know he needs a swift
embrace, someone to tell him fear is everyone's story.

No, I want him to hear my footsteps, so maybe he'll grasp
the ball tighter, face into that hit. Then mercy, swift
as memory, runs back and saves him from that story.

Saving Daylight

saving daylight
I wake early, find the stars
are out of place

୬

wanted: old porch
horses at pasture
loose shoes

୬

pouring coffee
in a white mug
I watch an eclipse

୬

misty lake—
a black branch
drifts by

୬

the carpenter
sketches a new house
on a 2x4

୬

fat raindrop
on a leaf of grass
almost

୬

vesper sparrow
or savannah
give me some song

❧

salamander
curls in the girl's hand—
faint smile

❧

canoe
all day I watch
her pale neck

❧

midsummer—
this rose tattoo
gets redder

❧

sunrise
on a tackling sled—
line of soldiers

❧

pickup truck
deer in the rusty bed
a fine rain

❧

cleaning the shotgun
oil stains
on my fingers

❧

O dust, O broom
O sweeper made of dust
O broom, O dust

✲

half-empty bottle
whiskey trembles
at a touch

✲

Indian summer
the tang of woodsmoke
sweeter now

✲

autumn afternoon—
mother touches
my thinning hair

✲

autumn dusk—
I've forgotten
who gave me this scar

✲

drowsy autumn
the kingfisher's blue
sharpens the sky

✲

a window
crows flash by
nightfall

❧

cold morning—
I find the flaws
in my house

❧

old dog
runs again
in her dreams

❧

hours before snow
the white
of the sycamore

❧

out of the endless
winter clouds
a snowflake

❧

snowflakes
on a black windshield
the stars fade

❧

falling snow—
furnace clatter
the only talk

❧

New Year's Eve—
raccoons
topple trash cans

❧

raw wind
through the mountains—
what are you are you

❧

with my daughter
reading of Issa
without his

❧

lifting firewood
I find my wife's silk bra
in my shirtsleeve

❧

the whiteness
as she lifts her shirt
moonlit snow

❧

after lovemaking
starlight touches us
from afar

❧

cooking
mid-blizzard
I add more curry

❧

clouds racing
a sundog
disappears

꙳

I take off my glove
to show my daughter
the Pleiades

꙳

a crow leaps
from the bare branch—
spring morning

꙳

outside Goodwill
a new pair of old jeans
and the blue sky

꙳

for sale sign
a chrysalis
hangs from the frame

꙳

long after the wind
pines along the mountain hold
the shape of the wind

Bathing

The candles lit, I let you down in water
at first too hot to bathe in, watching how
you sit up out of the tub and would rather
I not wait or, hopeless, look down
amid steam to where your hands lather
your belly, taut as apple skin. And though
you watch me as you wash, it doesn't matter
that I'm here. Your eyes won't let me through.

Just once, I hope, you'll break the filmy surface
with your knee, water beading from your skin
like dew from an orange. And so your face
meets mine, I'll touch the tracks where water lines
your long leg, hold your knee as if to mend
the cuts we couldn't wash, the many times.

For Shannon Wiegmann

The Thread

I lift a long hair from the book
I'm reading. How close a life can seem.
Around two fingers I wind
its brown, kinked length,
like the loop of mending thread
a tailor sews
in the breast of his winter coat.

A Blessing

This day, by the creek's edge,
I trace what water allows me
to see: gold pebbles, a shoal
of minnows, soda cans faded
to ghostly green. A tree swallow
perches the gray, scarcely leafed
branches of a cottonwood, watching
over me. Restless, I came down
to this sandy bank and light hard
as glass, looking for the words
they might offer in blessing
a marriage of friends. I met
only stillness, quiet, the creek
purling at its own patient speed.
That's how it should be. We don't bless,
but come into this presence to be
blessed. Above, branches tangle
into a vault. The swallow, a shard
of stained glass, chitters and darts
away. That's how it is. The creekbed
glints in the light as the light
falls constant upon the water.

For Alycia Bergen and Kyle Thompson

For a Joining of Hands

Every fall we long again
for completion, for rain to soften
the parched, stubbled fields,
for snow to glaze dark creekbanks.
At evening, whippoorwills call
their names each to each,
while deer, grown fat and musky
for the rut, come together
in a clash of antlers, dance
beneath gold and bloodred leaves.

Fallen, we want to be married to this world,
to open ourselves and be set free,
as poplars unfurl moist wings
from leaf-scars in their branches,
or the shagbark hickory, toppled
by January ice, softens, rots,
then blossoms in spring with molds
brilliant as blown embers.
How simple this place, this life
would be, if only we knew to listen.

Tonight, a man and a woman,
strangers once, call softly to each other.
They desire to be joined forever,
their hands tangled like forest roots.
It can be, yes, and it can never be.
The rings they give cannot be worn
without that emptiness at the center.
Who would join forever, will one day
be asked to let go, to set free. It is
the love we were born for, a strange music

that comes to us, sometimes, in fragments.

For Susan & Ted Dimitry

Epithalamion with Charles Mingus's *Black Saint and the Sinner Lady* Playing Through It

Love doesn't want an explanation, but hungers
for music to set it on the path of righteousness,

so start with a precise, midrange tempo, the theme played
over and over, as if the band were trying to get it right,

as if the song were a lovers' quarrel about the best place to
    live:
a small valley that feels big, where you can raise donkeys,

or a great good place with the Harmony Bar nearby,
soul food and Charles Mingus on the jukebox,

where Mingus's *Black Saint and the Sinner Lady* is playing
    even now,
sublime sounds spliced with outtakes and overdubs—

in one recording, you hear Mingus shouting at the pianist
to *Play the right song!*— then that broken melody

graces you back into time, back into the great good life
you've been trying to live all along, not by yourself,

but with this other, this beloved, for each is beloved as the
    other,
and the song's an hour-and-a-half conversation

in an Upper East Side coffee shop, where for once the talk
    is not
about work or school, books or movies, but about the two
    of you,

the warm, cadenced voice that pulls people close,
the soft hair smooth as the wood of an old jazz guitar,

a talk so good you write down every word on a cocktail
    napkin
you never throw away, flimsy flag of the heart's surrender,

so that now, at the end, when the band comes back
to the theme that got it started, the arrangement's the same

notes in the same places, a reminder that love must stick
with the path it makes in life—*Play the right song!*—

but underneath that repetition, one cosmic difference: O
    Beloved,
once you've mastered the theme, you can riff it even
    sweeter than before.

For Helen Hoguet and David Lacroix

Timor Domini

It is not fear of the Lord, but of the body
that is the beginning of wisdom.
The way a horse's heart surges into her
tongue licking salt from your hand,
or a piss outdoors in winter leaves you
so cold you weave both arms about your shoulders.
The absolutely absolute. In the courtyard
of the Franciscan monastery in Toledo,
I watched my wife beneath an orange tree
that bore oranges perfect as her breasts.
That will bear them after. A fact
that must be swallowed to make it all perfect.
The world the sacrament of itself.

Two Trees

I. Maple

When God spoke tree,
it was a maple branched
from the tossing winds
of his voice that day:
gray bark, delicately scored,
leaves like a fox track
or a child's outspread hand,
and sap that boils and boils away
to a sweetness so heavy
the tongue becomes a root
in the dark earth, drinking
snowmelt and spring showers.
So perfectly tree,
                so full of shade,
we almost fail to notice them,
till each fall they unfurl
in flame.

II. Birches

Call them ghosts if you like,
call them fingerbones jutting from dirt.
These trees say there is no death,
say the soul's for no one's keeping
but breaks open
in snowy bark, silver leaves, green shade
season after season.
Birches divide into three trunks
the way a woman with child
is herself divided
between mother, child,
and the strange being they make together,
whose life doesn't last a year,
who dies at the moment of birth

and is raised
the next instant
as two bodies, incorruptible, forever.

For Agnes and Adeline Potter

Say This

Say it's the first spring of your child's life.
Say the cherries have blossomed pink and white,
the sky pale blue. Say you look at your wife:
there's not an inch of her doesn't delight
your every glance, every breath, every touch.
But it's been so long since you just watched her.
New fears, new dreams. Your world has changed so much
the woods outside, bright with finch and flower,
can't even compare. Say you stroke her face
this moment your lovely child is asleep,
hold the curve of her jaw in your rough hand.
This is the love you both wished for. You keep
quiet, just looking, longing, but your heart says
all she is: wife, mother, godsend, God's end.

The Basket

Grasping no other recourse
under our time's accursed edict,
Every child that is born, throw into the Nile,
I lay my daughter in this basket
of papyrus, new-made, smooth,
secured in inky grammar of pitch and bitumen,
a crib, the best I could make,
for to lose my child to the world.

If word from the great house charges
my progeny to face judgment in the current,
I'll yet guile them,
not with fabulous camouflage
or the distraction of worldly matters
paid the gatekeepers that I, night-covered,
might sneak her to safety.

No, this basket
which I drift on the whims and wonders
of our protean river,
this basket is supple and strong,
diving with the flumes,
slipping the snaps of sedentary crocodiles
grown fat on vibrant pearls
borne to them along the current,
resisting the sticky soil of sedgeways,
and gently silencing her cries
lest some vicious, fleeting beast
or no one come.

And if she survives,
I'll never know the games she plays,
tend her cuts even as she cuts back,
watch her grow only to part.
No, the parting comes now,
early, dangerous,
because my world works this way, our world

a place no child should live to see
because all our children
have been ordered drowned by it.

But all this accomplishes nothing
unless she is found,
shored among reeds and fuzzy cattails
(tired from crying perhaps),
by some pharaoh's son,
who'll pay a Hebrew woman to milk her,
draw her to righteousness
even as he drew her from the water, tenderly,
and love her as her own father
might if he could.

The Wreck We're Passing

Daughter, don't look. Let darkness
drift ribbons over your eyes.
The wreck we're passing wants to burn
itself into a memory,
into memory. Lean back, listen
while I speak these lines to you.

The startle of blue jays in leaves
is the only harshness you'll ever know.
Night is a quiet boat, whose motions
will gently rock you under stars.

You'll never be afraid while I am
close by, and if this proves untrue,
remember a father's lies
carry far, passports to a distant land.

For Isabelle Cone

Beauty

Life has many terms
it asks us to uphold
if we are to go on living.
Beauty has but one condition:
we must be dying to see it.

What the gods envisioned
when they pursued their rapes
as swans or showers of gold
wasn't beauty, but the hope
they might possess it and survive.

They never glimpsed the mortals
afterwards: Leda, trembling
like an aspen leaf above a stream,
Danae caressing, then beating
the taut skin of her belly.

But someone brought a blanket,
offered tea, blew the fire awake
and led them to sit close beside.
Someone knew: the divine devastates,
but there is a life that follows.

So beauty begins when storms pass,
springwater clears, and leaves
unfurling gather the breeze.
If this is too gentle a thought for you,
perhaps you have yet to be broken,

the tough nut waiting to crack.

That Singing in the Darkness

All your grown life, you believe
if there's nothing else
certain and sweet,
there's always summer peaches,
tough-skinned, then soft and yielding.
Even the ochre, crenellated pith
waiting at the heart
is factual,
hard and fierce as sunlight
on a morning you wake alone,
the bed chill
as a bier of marble.
Who doesn't crave certainty,
even if it breaks your teeth,
that stone
buried like a storm in the sunset-
hued flesh of a peach?
It's something you can count on—
after a little sweetness
each day brings
a little hardness at the core.
Then, one afternoon, you're standing
at a table, peach on a plate,
knife in hand,
and you slice down through
the peach's peel,
its fruit,
its stone.
Two halves reveal
the mystery
of a seed already growing,
smooth fiber pale as an almond,
the first shoot piercing
the tough seed you thought was worthless.
You don't eat such fruit.
You bury it with your hands
in the black soil

of a garden.
It isn't even fruit anymore.
It's what bears fruit,
the tree your tongue tastes
in the summer juice.
You plant it in the soil
so it can keep growing,
so it can go on singing in the darkness.

The Broken Meadow

There are only a few ways
of making your way in this fallen world,
as the ways of writing a poem
are few, and equally desperate.
You can trifle with words and hope,
like the hognose snake
with its excited hiss and venomless bite,
you won't have to mean
what you say.
                        You can rail
against restraint or freedom,
shout down the patterns that measure
your days, or lament their loss.
You can choose not to write,
a gutsy call, though not
the same as choosing not to live.
Or you may lie still
in partial fullness,
                        a meadow
ploughed open and left
to papuses blown from miles around.
Such variegated fields blossom,
fall back, grow again,
drawing bees and finches
to buck pollen and scatter seed.
Only a horse or two browse there,
turned out by the farmer
who first cut, then abandoned the soil.
In the end, what belongs belongs:
closing dark, slants of light,
a broken meadow
                            speaking to the sky
in tongues of wildflower and long grass.